Winter Blues

Weavers from England, Ireland, and Scotland

THE FOSTER AND MURIEL MCCARL

COVERLET GALLERY

SAINT VINCENT COLLEGE

Winter Blues

Weavers from England, Ireland, and Scotland

THE FOSTER AND MURIEL MCCARL

COVERLET GALLERY

SAINT VINCENT COLLEGE

AUTHOR
Lauren M. Lamendola, Curator

DESIGN
Jordan Hainsey

CONTENTS

INTRODUCTION

The McCarl Coverlet Collection is made up of a colorful assortment of textiles woven by weavers of many different traditions and backgrounds. Weavers from England, Ireland, and Scotland created coverlets woven in a double weave style. This technique featured two sets of warps woven together to create two pieces of cloth joined together. They were generally woven with blue and white threads. This technique was not unanimously used by weavers from these regions, as you will see throughout the book, but it does dominate weavings from these regions.

Foster and Muriel McCarl
&
Their Collection

The prized collection of antique American coverlets owned by Foster and Muriel McCarl was gifted to Saint Vincent College in 2004. The Beaver Falls couple conveyed its collection of over 300 coverlets to the College along with funds for the care and preservation of one of the premier coverlet collections in the country. Selections from the collection are permanently displayed at the Fred M. Rogers Center on the Saint Vincent College campus.

A love of American history led the McCarls to purchase their first historic coverlet in 1959. That began what has become one of the finest collections of American coverlets in the Country and largest in the world. Foster McCarl recalled the joy that he and his wife experienced over the years in assembling the collection, learning from reference books about the prized acquisitions, and developing friendships with dealers and other collectors who shared their interest.

"Muriel and I both love American history which led us to antiques," Foster McCarl has said. "Not just coverlets, but quilts, furniture, iron, brass, china, pottery, wooden ware, etc. The first antique we bought was an Elkington silver-plated tea and coffee service in July of 1955. We each were attracted to different items, and I think that that made our collecting more interesting."

The couple bought their first two coverlets in August 1959 in Ephrata, Pennsylvania; three months later they bought five more coverlets, and the collection was begun. Mr. McCarl has written about his special interest in these historic items. "Someone asked me, 'why coverlets?' My response was 'Where else can you find an item that has the name of the weaver who created it by hand, the name of the person it was woven for, the date and

the community where the work was completed? When you have a coverlet with all this information, you have found an indisputable piece of American history.'"

These 19th century bed coverlets, which are woven with intricate patterns in vibrant colors of red, blue, white and green, were woven almost exclusively by professional male weavers, usually in the Middle Atlantic states and the Midwest, and were affordable enough for middle-class, rural Americans. Described as "figured and fancy," these coverlets were most popular between 1824 and the Civil War, and reflect the Victorian sensibilities of the past, offering intricate designs with a wealth of flowers, trees and popular patriotic emblems. Usually woven from a blend of cotton and wool, coverlets were often commissioned for particular occasions such as a marriage or birth. The names of the weaver and recipient, as well as the location and date, were often woven into the corner blocks. With that information, coverlets help tell the stories of the people who made and used them, and serve as a springboard to studying craftsmanship and history.

English
Weavers

DANIEL STEPHENSON
IOWA

Daniel Stephenson was born in 1823 in England. As a child, he was apprenticed to his father who was a weaver by trade. As the economic situation in England for hand weavers declined due to the invention of the power loom, Stephenson and his father immigrated to America. They arrived in 1840 and began to try to make their fortunes weaving in New York. It took the two of them about three years to make enough money to send for Stephenson's mother and five siblings. When his father moved to Ohio, Stephenson went to Canada with a friend and became temporarily employed as a lumberjack. After this, it is believed that he was apprenticed to either Dennis Cosley or Robert Crossley. Stephenson relocated to Fairfield, Iowa, around 1849 and he married his first wife, Mary Ellen Dodson, in 1852. When the Civil War broke out, he began weaving coverlets for the Union Army. Stephenson died of stomach cancer in 1892.

Stephenson wove in the tied-biederwand style which is uncharacteristic of English weavers who usually created bi-colored double woven coverlets. This particular Stephenson coverlet is a navy, red, and natural tied-biederwand coverlet with fringe on three sides. The centerfield has a double rose motif and is bordered by a pattern of snowflakes and pine trees.

2008.1.36

DAVID
INGHAM
LEROY
TOWNSHIP
BRADFORD
COUNTY
1852
W. CRATER

12

David Ingham emigrated from his birthplace in England in 1828 and settled in Bradford County, Pennsylvania. He worked with his brother, Joseph, at the Monroeton Woolen factory. It is believed that he wove coverlets from 1847 until 1868. Weaving was most likely his second profession as he is listed in Pennsylvania Census records as a head of household engaged in manufacturing and trades as well as a farmer.

The blue and white coloring of this Ingham coverlet is very typical of English weavings; however, its tied-beiderwand structure is more commonly found among Germanic weavers. The centerfield contains a double rose and floral pattern. This coverlet actually has two borders; the inner grapevine pattern is bordered by a thin line of geometric shapes. There is fringe on one side only.

2008.1.166

14

Samuel Graham
Image courtsey of Heinz County Historical Society Museum

Samuel Graham was born on July 11, 1805, in Manchester, England. He left England when he was about 18 years old. He landed in New York and married an American woman in Philadelphia. After that, he settled in the late 1830s in New Castle, Henry County, Indiana. There, he began weaving. Some of his coverlets proclaimed Zachary Taylor's nickname, "Rough and Ready," which was one of his presidential campaign slogans. Interestingly, Graham's usual corner block included an eagle, rather than the traditional English lion. He set up his weaving business, and possibly his residence, in an old log building that was formerly used as the courthouse of New Castle. Graham's business flourished, and in 1840 he purchased a forty acre plot of land in Indiana. He continued to amass land and wealth throughout his lifetime and was quite a prosperous weaver. During the American Civil War, he took his wife, Elizabeth, and their children back to England. They returned to Indiana after the war, and it is possible that he did not weave when he came back. He is listed in the 1870 census as a retired weaver. Unlike many of his weaving counterparts, he did not engage in a secondary profession, and at the time of his death in 1871, his estate was valued at $34,000 (roughly $600,000 today.)

2008.1.13

Woven in 1854 in New Castle, Indiana, this navy and white double woven coverlet has a lovely pattern. The carpet medallion centerfield is bordered by a stylized fern and flower pattern on the bottom and a bird of paradise border on the left and right side. Graham's urn with a flower corner block became his trademark pattern after 1850.

This 1848 coverlet is another creation of Samuel Graham. Made of navy wool and natural cotton, it boasts an intricate carpet medallion centerfield. The right and left borders are composed of a bird of paradise design while the bottom is edged by an oak leaf motif. The eagle on a branch trademark is occasionally found in Graham's handiwork and can be observed in all but one of the weaver's coverlets in the McCarl Collection.

2008.1.85

18

It is rather uncommon to find a coverlet with the extensive detail as incorporated in this beautiful coverlet woven by Samuel Graham. The blue and white coloring is very typical; however, the carpet medallion centerfield accented with tiny pin dots is a rare find. The side borders are also extraordinarily detailed and unique, consisting of both loose and potted flower images. The bottom oak leaf border is common throughout Graham's weavings.

2008.1.238

20

In classic Graham style, this coverlet features an eagle corner block dated 1842. A signature carpet medallion centerfield fills the spread of the coverlet. The pattern is bordered on the left and right by a fern and flower border and by an oak leaf border on the bottom edge.

2008.1.301

Irish Weavers

24

James Alexander was born on November 2, 1770, in Belfast, Ireland, to parents of Scottish descent. In 1797, Alexander left Ireland and immigrated to America. He settled down near Little Britain, New York, located in Orange County, and began farming and weaving. He married Catharine Bullard in 1800, and the two of them set up house in a log cabin on the farm. When the family outgrew the cabin, Alexander built a frame house and converted the cabin into a weaving studio. Alexander was trained in an Irish weaving guild and he brought the trade with him to America. Alexander was one of the earliest figured and fancy coverlet weavers in the United States. In fact, according to records, he was weaving in the style prior to any other weaver documented in the country. He specialized in double woven coverlets which he dubbed "flowert" coverlets in the early 1820s. He charged between $2.00 and $5.50 for a coverlet. Alexander took up a variety of other odd jobs in order to make ends meet when he did not have weaving work. Alexander died in 1870, just a few months shy of 100 years.

This double woven coverlet has a rose medallion centerfield and is bordered on the side by monkeys, spread-winged eagles, and pillars topped with Masonic symbols. The bottom border has a repeating pattern of buildings and spread-winged eagles. The corner blocks read "American Independence Declared July 4, 1776 Wove in 1840 L. Hotis."

2008.1.168

26

WILLIAM LUNN
OHIO

William Lunn was born in 1787 in Ireland. It is unknown when he left his homeland and immigrated to the United States, but he began weaving in Ohio in 1832. Census records place him in Muskingum County, Ohio, by 1840. He wove for only a short period of time, and there are only seven known Lunn coverlets. While his coverlets are dated, they do not include a location.

This McCarl coverlet exemplifies one of two centerfield patterns used by Lunn. The weaver's name is present throughout the centerfield along with the date and the letters SEAFL which is short for "Seaflower," the coverlet pattern's name. The coverlet is bordered on all four sides. The top and bottom borders contain a repeating six petaled flower design which is repeated in the centerfield of the coverlet. The side borders contain an alternating floral pattern and the letters "CS."

2008.1.167

Scottish Weavers

30

ROBERT ALEXANDER
OHIO

According to Robert Alexander's grandson, Alexander was born in 1801 in Kilmarnock, Scotland, where he learned the weaving trade while working in a shawl factory in Paisley, Scotland. He immigrated to Thompsonville, Connecticut, in 1840 where he worked in a carpet mill. In 1849, Alexander, his wife Mary, and their family moved to Canfield, Ohio, where he began weaving coverlets. According to census records, it is possible that Alexander may have come to America earlier than 1840, as there is evidence that his eldest daughter, Mary, was born in Connecticut in 1833. Robert Alexander continued to reside in Ohio until his death in 1880.

Robert Alexander did not date his coverlets, but he did include his name and the location in his corner blocks. There are six recorded centerfields and five different borders used by Alexander. All of his coverlets contain a bottom border that depict a series of horsemen and their dogs. The side borders in this particular coverlet contain architectural buildings. Alexander used four varying borders with architectural details and one that contained a peacock pattern. The centerfield in this coverlet contains a medallion motif of two tulips, two roses, and foliage as the primary pattern. The secondary patterns have a diamond shape and are placed between the larger medallions.

2008.1.169

32

JAMES CRAIG
INDIANA

Wool Coverlet on loan from the private collection of John Simmermaker

James Craig, also known as Canada Jim, was born in Ayrshire, Scotland, in 1819. He left Scotland in 1845 with his wife, Margaret, and arrived in Canton, Indiana, by way of Canada. He was most likely a distant cousin of William Craig, Sr., but had no professional or known personal relationship with the Craig family weavers in Indiana. By 1852, he was well established in Canton. He formed a partnership with Matthew Young, and the two wove together until 1864, when Craig moved to Brazil, Indiana. Young was Craig's brother-in-law, and he emigrated from Scotland in 1852 to join Craig in the weaving business. At the time of Young's arrival, Craig purchased a farm and with the extra help in the weaving enterprise, he was able to split his time between the weaving shop and the farm. Craig passed away in 1896 in Brazil, Indiana.

34

JAMES CUNNINGHAM
NEW YORK

James Cunningham was born in Scotland in 1797, and he settled in New Hartford, New York, around 1820. He formed a weaving partnership with Samuel Butterfield, and the pair worked together until 1835. Cunningham/Butterfield coverlets were typically not signed or dated. After the partnership ended, Cunningham continued weaving alone. He married three times and he produced eleven children out of the partnerships. Cunningham died after 1865, but his date of death is unknown.

Cunningham used two dominant corner block patterns in his weaving: "Washington on Horseback" and "Excelsior." This blue and white double weave "Washington on Horseback" is an excellent example of Cunningham's most popular design. This coverlet is also unique because its centerfield is not symmetrical. There are four medallions in the centerfield, but the top two are smaller, condensed versions of the bottom medallions. A secondary motif of leaves and flowers are arranged between the medallions, and smaller shapes fill in the empty space. The center pattern is bordered by eagles holding arrows and laurel leaves in their talons. Wilted sunflowers are positioned between the eagles on the top and bottom borders while the side borders contains flowers and floral arrangements between the eagles. The corner block depicts Washington on horseback. The coverlet is dated 1845 and reads, "UNITED WE STAND DIVIDED WE FALL UNDER THIS WE PROSPER."

2008.1.284

36

Cunningham's second most popular pattern is found in this double weave "Excelsior" coverlet. The centerfield is dominated by a large four medallion design. The corner blocks of the pattern feature Lady Liberty with a torch and Lady Justice with a scale flanking an eagle perched on a shield. The name "Excelsior" comes from the motto of New York which means "ever upward." The corner block pattern is the weaver's rendition of the New York state coat of arms which was officially adopted in 1778.

2008.1.83

WOVEN AT THE ITHACA CARPET FACTORY, BY A. DAVIDSON. 1842.

ARCHIBALD DAVIDSON
NEW YORK

Archibald Davidson was born in 1771 in Scotland where he was trained as a weaver. It is unknown when he arrived in America, but records indicate that one of his sons was born in Pennsylvania in 1805, and four others were born in New Jersey between 1809 and 1818. We do not know how long he stayed in either of those states, but he began weaving in Ithaca, New York, in 1830. His shop was a quarter mile outside of Ithaca, and he often advertised his wares to the citizens of the town. Davidson's advertisements boasted the quality of the work and assured that his weavings would last twice as long as any factory made cloth. He and his wife, Jane, were devout Scotch Presbyterians and were well known within their community. The family stayed in Ithaca until the 1850s when they moved to Warsaw, New York.

This 1842 Davidson masterpiece is woven of blue wool and white cotton. The centerfield is filled with an intricate motif of bird and floral medallions. Three sides of the coverlet are bordered by a repeating floral pattern that features a large floral medallion flanked by two smaller flowers and a bird of paradise on either side. The coverlet reads, "Woven at the Ithaca Carpet Factory." The coverlet contains two corner blocks and has no fringe.

2008.1.4

40

The second Davidson coverlet in the McCarl Collection features his "Liberty and Independence" design. The blue and white double woven coverlet has a repeating double rose medallion centerfield accented by tiny stars. The bottom border features horses and an eagle holding a shield and an arrow topped by nine stars.

2008.1.52

42

John A. Gamble was born in 1813 in Scotland. Not much is known about Gamble other than he immigrated to America sometime in the early 1830s and settled in Blair Township, Pennsylvania. By 1850, he had relocated to Potter Township, Pennsylvania, with his wife, Jane. He moved once again to Edgemont, Pennsylvania, where he lived out the rest of his days.

Gamble's 1835 double woven coverlet is constructed of burnt orange wool, navy blue wool, and white cotton. The colors overlap to create a third mauve color within the pattern. A block pattern consisting of three square designs make up the centerfield while the border is adorned with trees, flowers, and perched eagles.

2008.1.70

44

JOHN HOLMES
NEW YORK

John Holmes was born in Paisley, Scotland in, 1757 and came to New York City in 1817 with his wife, Ann ,as well as his two sons, John Jr. and Walter. He found his way to Delhi in Delaware County and with the help of friends, settled into a piece of land about three miles north of present day DeLancy, New York. Holmes affectionately names his land "Holmes Hollow." Holmes was one of three famed weavers who wove the highly prized "Delhi Coverlets." The other two Delhi weavers were Asahel Amora Phelps and John Benjamin Phelps II. Holmes was well trained in Scotland and is credited with introducing the flying shuttle into Delaware County. His work spans from 1832 to 1834, but it is believed that he continued weaving until his death on April 14, 1839.

Delhi coverlets have several distinguishing features. Most of them are blue and white in color, although there are several red versions in existence. All of the Dehli coverlets are woven in the double weave style which was common among Irish, English, and Scottish weavers. The Delhi coverlets are not fringed and they have similar centerfield patterns. It is common for Delhi coverlets to have three medallions across the centerfield and four down the length of the textile. John Holmes used a signature pinwheel and the date in his corner blocks, as can be seen in this example from the McCarl Collection.

2008.1.87

45